KEY FACTS

for

NEW BELIEVERS

Dag Heward-Mills

Parchment House

Unless otherwise stated, all Scripture quotations are taken from the King James Version of the Bible.

KEY FACTS FOR NEW BELIEVERS

Copyright © 2017 Dag Heward-Mills

First published 2017 by Parchment House
2nd Printing 2018

Find out more about Dag Heward-Mills at:

Healing Jesus Campaign
Email: evangelist@daghewardmills.org
Website: www.daghewardmills.org
Facebook: Dag Heward-Mills
Twitter: @EvangelistDag

ISBN : 978-1-68398-268-5

Contents

CHAPTER 1

How to Become a Born-Again Christian

If you want to be born again, you must do two important things:

i.   **You must first believe in Jesus Christ as the Son of God.**

Whosoever believeth that Jesus is the Christ is born of God:...

1 John 5:1

ii. **Secondly, you must ask Him to come into your heart and your life. You must say a prayer like this and mean it from the bottom of your heart:**

"Lord Jesus, I come to You as a sinner, lost and condemned to Hell. I repent of my sins and ask for Your forgiveness. I believe with all my heart that You died on the cross and rose up again for my sins. I open my heart to You and receive You as my Lord and personal Saviour. Please take control of my life and make me what You want me to be. From today, I am Yours and You are mine. Thank You, Father for this wonderful gift of salvation, Amen."

What Happens When You Become Born Again?

The Spirit of God will come upon you, and into your heart. Then the inner part of you will be born or produced again.

God gives you a new heart and spirit altogether!

A new heart also will I give you, and a new spirit will I put within you: and I will take away the stony heart out of your flesh, and I will give you an heart of flesh.

And I will put my spirit within you, and cause you to walk in my statutes, and ye shall keep my judgments, and do them.

Ezekiel 36:26-27

With your new spirit, you become a new man or a new creature. You are ready to live a new life. This new life is possible because you are actually a new person with a new heart.

To be born again is as simple as that. People want to do complicated things. But becoming born again is very simple!

Who Then Is a Born-Again Christian?

A born-again Christian is someone who has personally received Jesus Christ into his life and is determined to live a life controlled by the Word of God and under the guidance of the Spirit of God.

CHAPTER 2

Key Facts about Salvation

N ow that you are born again it is important to fully understand your new life in Christ and build up on what God has begun in your life.

8 Important Key Facts You Must Know

1. **The Bible says that we human beings are sinners (by birth and by our lives).**

   For ALL HAVE SINNED, and come short of the glory of God;...

   > Romans 3:23

2. **The Bible teaches that the good things we do are seen as filthy rags that cannot please God.**

   But we are all as an unclean thing, and ALL OUR RIGHTEOUSNESSES ARE AS FILTHY RAGS;...

   > Isaiah 64:6

3. **We can never be holy enough because we were conceived in sin.**

Behold, I WAS SHAPEN IN INIQUITY; and in sin did my mother conceive me.

Psalm 51:5

4. The Bible tells us that none of us can receive salvation by doing anything in particular.

For by grace are ye saved through faith; and that not of yourselves:...

Ephesians 2:8

5. We are not saved by our good works but by our faith in Christ.

That if thou shalt confess with thy mouth the Lord Jesus, and shalt believe in thine heart that God hath raised him from the dead, thou shalt be saved.

Romans 10:9

6. God will definitely punish the sins of men with curses, sicknesses and separation from God (both now and forever in the lake of fire).

But the fearful, and unbelieving, and the abominable, and murderers, and whoremongers, and sorcerers, and idolaters, and all liars, shall have their part in the lake which burneth with fire and brimstone which is the second death.

Revelation 21:8

7. There are two reasons why God decided to save us:

i. The first reason why God decided to save us is that He loves His creation very much.

For God so loved the world, that he gave his only begotten Son, that whosoever believeth in him should not perish, but have everlasting life.

John 3:16

ii. **The second reason why God decided to save us is that we could not save ourselves through good deeds like church membership, religion and our own righteousness.**

But we are all as an unclean thing, and all our righteousnesses are as filthy rags;...

Isaiah 64:6

8. **Jesus Christ had to come and die on the cross for us because the Bible teaches that without the shedding of blood, there is no forgiveness of sins.**

And almost all things are by the law purged with blood; and without shedding of blood is no remission.

Hebrews 9:22

CHAPTER 3

Six Powerful Results of Your Salvation

Now that you have given your life to Jesus Christ, you have become born again. You have now received these blessings from the Lord:

1. **All your sins—past and present ones are forgiven by Jesus' sacrifice. Your future sins will also be forgiven if you confess them.**

   If we confess our sins, he is faithful and just to forgive us our sins, and to cleanse us from all unrighteousness.

   1 John 1:9

2. **You have received eternal life.**

   Verily, verily, I say unto you, He that heareth my word, and believeth on him that sent me, hath everlasting life,...

   John 5:24

3.   You are now a child of God.

But as many as received him, to them gave he power to become the sons of God,...

John 1:12

4.   You are now a new creation in Christ.

Therefore if any man be in Christ, he is a new creature: old things are passed away; behold, all things are become new.

2 Corinthians 5:17

5.   Your name is written in Heaven in the Lamb's Book of Life.

And there shall in no wise enter into it any thing that defileth, neither whatsoever worketh abomination, or maketh a lie: but they which are written in the Lamb's book of life.

Revelation 21:27

6.   You will go to Heaven, The New Jerusalem.

And the city had no need of the sun, neither of the moon, to shine in it: for the glory of God did lighten it, and the Lamb is the light thereof. And the nations of them which are saved shall walk in the light of it: and the kings of the earth do bring their glory and honour into it.

Revelation 21:23-24

CHAPTER 4

What You Must Know About Water Baptism

1. Baptism comes from the Greek word "baptiso" which means "immersion". Water baptism is therefore the immersion of a person totally into water. It is not sprinkling or pouring of water.

    And Jesus, when he was baptized, went up straightway OUT OF THE WATER:...

    Matthew 3:16

    And John also was baptizing in Aenon near to Salim, BECAUSE THERE WAS MUCH WATER THERE: and they came, and were baptized.

    John 3:23

    A lot of water is needed for baptism by immersion.

2. Water baptism is a command to anyone who becomes born again.

    And he said unto them, Go ye into all the world, and preach the gospel to every creature. He that believeth and is baptized shall be saved; but he that believeth not shall be damned.

    Mark 16:15-16

3. **Water baptism is a direct act of obedience to Christ's instruction.**

    He that believeth and is baptized shall be saved; but he that believeth not shall be damned.

    Mark 16:16

4. **Baptism is not for church membership, but an open declaration of our new stand in Christ.**

    For as many of you as have been baptized into Christ have put on Christ.

    Galatians 3:27

    When you are baptized you are openly declaring that you have by faith "put on Christ" so that men may see Christ in you.

5. **We identify with the death, burial and resurrection of our Lord Jesus Christ in baptism.**

    Therefore we are buried with him by baptism into death: that like as Christ was raised up from the dead by the glory of the Father, even so we also should walk in newness of life.

    Romans 6:4

    The lowering of the convert completely under the water pictures Christ's death; the submersion of the convert speaks of His burial and the raising of the convert from the water signifies His resurrection.

CHAPTER 5

The Baptism of the Holy Ghost

What is the baptism of the Holy Ghost? The baptism of the Holy Ghost is an experience the believer receives after being born again. It is a promise from God to all those who believe in Jesus Christ.

John the Baptist gave witness of Christ before His baptism that:

> **I indeed baptize you with water unto repentance: but he that cometh after me is mightier than I, whose shoes I am not worthy to bear: he shall baptize you with the Holy Ghost, and with fire:**
>
> **Matthew 3:11**

What Happens When a Person Receives the Baptism of the Holy Ghost?

The initial sign that you are baptized with the Holy Ghost is that you speak in tongues.

> **And when the day of Pentecost was fully come, they were all with one accord in one place.... And they**

were all filled with the Holy Ghost, and began to speak with other tongues, as the Spirit gave them utterance.

Acts 2:1-4

And when Paul had laid his hands upon them, the Holy Ghost came on them; and they spake with tongues, and prophesied.

Acts 19:6

Who Can Receive the Baptism of the Holy Ghost?

Anyone who is born again can receive the baptism of the Holy Ghost with the evidence of speaking in tongues.

And these signs shall follow them that believe; In my name shall they cast out devils; THEY SHALL SPEAK WITH NEW TONGUES;...

Mark 16:17

How to Receive the Baptism of the Holy Ghost

1. **Firstly, you must be born again.**

This is the most important qualification.

And these signs shall follow them that believe;...they shall speak with new tongues;

Mark 16:17

2. **Secondly, you must desire the Holy Spirit.**

Then Peter said unto them, Repent, and be baptized every one of you in the name of Jesus Christ for the remission of sins, and ye shall receive the gift of the Holy Ghost.

For the promise is unto you, and to your children, and to all that are afar off, even as many as the Lord our God shall call.

Acts 2:38-39

Although it is a promise for every believer, God expects you to desire the gift so that when He pours out this blessing on you, it will not go waste or unused.

But covet earnestly the best gifts;...

1 Corinthians 12:31

...desire spiritual gifts,...

1 Corinthians 14:1

3. **Pray and ask God to baptize you with the Holy Ghost.**

If ye then, being evil, know how to give good gifts unto your children: how much more shall your heavenly Father give the Holy Spirit to them that ask him?

Luke 11:13

4. **Exercise your faith by speaking out in tongues.**

God is not going to put a radio box in your stomach and switch it on and off. He expects you to speak out! You must step out in faith and God will honour that faith.

And they were all filled with the Holy Ghost, and began to speak with other tongues, as the Spirit gave them utterance.

Acts 2:4

Sometimes it is helpful to get a senior Christian to assist you by laying hands on you and praying along with you. This can greatly facilitate the process and eliminate doubt and fear.

And when Paul had laid his hands upon them, the Holy Ghost came on them; and they spake with tongues, and prophesied.

Acts 19:6

When you start speaking in tongues for the first time, it may sound like a baby learning to speak "gibberish" but the Holy Ghost will enable you.

5.   Once you start speaking in tongues, don't stop it. Keep on praying!

The Bible describes the speaking of tongues in two ways. First it as a:

i.   River that flows out of your belly:

In the last day, that great day of the feast, Jesus stood and cried, saying, If any man thirst, let him come unto me, and drink.   He that believeth on me, as the scripture hath said, out of his belly shall flow rivers of living water. (But this spake he of the Spirit, which they that believe on him should receive: for the Holy Ghost was not yet given; because that Jesus was not yet glorified.)

John 7:37-39

So let the river flow!!

It is also a:

ii.   Stammering tongue:

For with stammering lips and another tongue will he speak to this people.

Isaiah 28:11

Tongues often sound like the voice of a stammerer—"ba ba ba ba" or "ma ma ma ma". This is a unique characteristic of the heavenly language.

CHAPTER 6

Develop Yourself by Speaking in Tongues

10 Reasons Why Every Believer Must Speak in Tongues

1. Speaking in tongues is a promise to every believer.

    He that believeth and is baptized shall be saved; but he that believeth not shall be damned. And these signs shall follow them that believe; In my name shall they cast out devils; they shall speak with new tongues;

    Mark 16:16,17

2. Speaking in tongues helps you to pray according to the will of God.

    Likewise the Spirit also helpeth our infirmities: for we know not what we should pray for as we ought: but the Spirit itself maketh intercession for us with groanings which cannot be uttered.

    Romans 8:26

3. **Speaking in tongues builds you up to become a strong and powerful Christian.**

    But ye, beloved, building up yourselves on your most holy faith, praying in the Holy Ghost,

    Jude 1:20

4. **Speaking in tongues is talking to God directly in a language only He understands.**

    For he that speaketh in an unknown tongue speaketh not unto men, but unto God: for no man understandeth him; howbeit in the spirit he speaketh mysteries.

    1 Corinthians 14:2

5. **Speaking in tongues gives your spirit the opportunity to pray.**

    For if I pray in an unknown tongue, my spirit prayeth, but my understanding is unfruitful.

    1 Corinthians 14:14

6. **Speaking in tongues makes your spirit pray best about things concerning you.**

    Your spirit knows deeper things about yourself than any other part of you.

    For what man knoweth the things of a man, save the spirit of man which is in him? even so the things of God knoweth no man, but the Spirit of God.

    1 Corinthians 2:11

    Sometimes you may not understand what you are going through in order to pray meaningfully in your normal language. However, you can still pray very effectively in tongues because your spirit knows many things that your mind hasn't yet grasped. Therefore allow your spirit to pray!

7.   Speaking in tongues makes you pray for a long time.

You are not limited by language, vocabulary and how to express yourself and so you can pray for a long time.

> **For if I pray in an unknown tongue, my spirit prayeth, but my understanding is unfruitful.**
>
> 1 Corinthians 14:14

8.   Speaking in tongues is a better way to express thanks and appreciation to God.

> **Else when thou shalt bless with the spirit, how shall he that occupieth the room of the unlearned say Amen at thy giving of thanks, seeing he understandeth not what thou sayest? FOR THOU VERILY GIVEST THANKS WELL ...**
>
> 1 Corinthians 14:16,17

9.   Speaking in tongues makes you more aware of the power of Christ.

You will become bold as you become more and more aware of the power that is at work in the believer. You can stand boldly as a true witness for Jesus. You are fearless in the face of demonic activity and your faith to deal with them is firm.

> **But ye shall receive power, after that the Holy Ghost is come upon you: and ye shall be witnesses unto me both in Jerusalem, and in all Judaea, and in Samaria, and unto the uttermost part of the earth.**
>
> Acts 1:8

10.   Speaking in tongues makes you   become more conscious of the presence of the Holy Spirit in you as you continue to communicate with God in tongues.

The Holy Spirit is in us to help us. Being more aware of His presence helps you to develop a personal relationship with Him and engage His participation, contribution and influence in our lives.

And I will pray the Father, and he shall give you another Comforter, that he may abide with you for ever; Even the Spirit of truth; whom the world cannot receive, because it seeth him not, neither knoweth him: but ye know him; for he dwelleth with you, and shall be in you.

John 14:16-17

The Journey on the Ship

Why should you go to heaven without experiencing all the blessings promised to believers to help our Christian lives here on earth? It will be like a man who saved all he could and bought a ticket to go to New York on a ship. He managed to use the rest of his savings to buy a box of cabin biscuits and drink.

Throughout the journey he never mingled with the other passengers nor visited the restaurants, cinema halls, etc. He never used any of the facilities like the swimming pools, gyms and saloons.

He thought to himself, "I'm not rich. I can't afford all that! Some people are really blessed!" He would then retreat to his cabin to enjoy his cabin biscuits and drink.

A few days to the end of the journey the captain spotted the lonely traveller and asked why he had never seen him the whole time and whether he had any problems with the services they offered. He replied that from what he saw the services were excellent only he couldn't participate because he couldn't afford any. The captain's jaw dropped in utter amazement and shock – the reason? Everything on board was already paid for!

The price of the ticket covered every facility on the ship! The man did not know! He had suffered needless pain and hardship throughout the journey. How sad!!

Unfortunately, many Christians are just like this lonely traveller.

There are many things included in our "salvation ticket" but we are not enjoying them either because of ignorance or we refuse to accept them for ourselves.

Speaking in tongues is part of the salvation ticket! Rise up and flow in it!!!

CHAPTER 7

Grow in Your New Life by Reading the Bible Regularly

4 Important Facts about the Bible

1. **The Bible is God's Word to mankind.**

   All scripture is given by inspiration of God, and is profitable for doctrine, for reproof, for correction, for instruction in righteousness: That the man of God may be perfect, throughly furnished unto all good works.

   2 Timothy. 3:16,17

2. **God's Word gives us direction for our lives.**

   The Word of God guides us in what to say, what to do and where to go. All our decisions and actions must be based on this all-important book.

   Thy word is a lamp unto my feet, and a light unto my path.

   Psalm 119:105

3.   The Word of God helps to change our thinking and keeps us from the bad habits of our past like drinking, smoking, premarital and extra-marital sex, the practice of boyfriends/girlfriends, and other sins in our lives.

Wherewithal shall a young man cleanse his way? by taking heed thereto according to thy word.

Psalm 119:9

4.   God's Word will make you a strong believer.

As you feed on the Word you grow in the Lord. Your spirit will grow and you will understand spiritual things.

And now, brethren, I commend you to God, and to the word of his grace, which is able to build you up, and to give you an inheritance among all them which are sanctified.

Acts 20:32

But the natural man receiveth not the things of the Spirt of God: for they are foolishness unto him: neither can he know them, because they are spiritually discerned.

1 Corinthians 2:14

3 Things You Must Do with the Word of God

1.   Desire the Word.

Just as babies survive and grow as they feed on milk daily, born-again Christians must survive and grow by daily feeding on the Word of God.

As newborn babes, desire the sincere milk of the word, that ye may grow thereby:

1 Peter 2:2

2.   You must have a daily quiet time to read the Bible.

This book of the law shall not depart out of thy mouth; but thou shalt meditate therein day and night, that thou mayest observe to do according to all that is written therein: for then thou shalt make thy way prosperous, and then thou shalt have good success.

Joshua 1:8

Quiet time is a regular daily time you keep with the Lord. It is a personal, unhurried time in Bible reading and praying. Quiet time is a time that God communicates with you through His word and prayer. In the next chapter I will share with you seven effective ways to have a quiet time.

3.   Be determined to be a doer of the Word.

As a born-again Chrisitan, you must fully obey every aspect of the Word of God. You must change your life in accordance to whatever the Bible says.

But be ye doers of the word, and not hearers only, deceiving your own selves. For if any be a hearer of the word, and not a doer, he is like unto a man beholding his natural face in a glass: For he beholdeth himself, and goeth his way, and straightway forgetteth what manner of man he was. But whoso looketh into the perfect law of liberty, and continueth therein, he being not a forgetful hearer, but a doer of the work, this man shall be blessed in his deed.

James 1:22-25

CHAPTER 8

Seven Steps to an Effective Quiet Time

Step 1: Pray to begin your Quiet Time.

I t's time to give the Lord praise and worship for His goodness. Pray and thank the Lord for another day. Thank Him for who He is, what He has done and what He can and will do. Now ask God to speak to you.

And the Lord passed by before him, and proclaimed, The Lord, The Lord God, merciful and gracious, longsuffering, and abundant in goodness and truth, Keeping mercy for thousands, forgiving iniquity and transgression and sin, and that will by no means clear the guilty; visiting the iniquity of the fathers, upon the children, and upon the children's children, unto the third and to the fourth generation. And Moses made haste, and bowed his head toward the earth, and worshipped.

Exodus 34:6-8

Step 2: Read a passage from the Bible expecting God to speak to you.

Open thou mine eyes, that I may behold wondrous things out of thy law.

Psalm 119:18

Read the passage for the day expecting God to speak to you from it. There are several ways of choosing your daily Bible reading passage.

How to Choose a Bible-Reading Passage for Your Quiet Time

a. Choose a book from the Bible of which you read a few verses every day. You must always remember where you ended so you can continue from the same place on the next day. In the New Testament, I have had wonderful quiet times as I have read through the books of Luke and Ephesians. In the Old Testament, I have also had wonderful quiet times as I have read through the books of Genesis and 1st and 2nd Samuel.

b. Choose a personality from the Bible whose life story you follow. A few verses from passages about Moses will give you much revelation for your life. You must always remember where you end your reading so that you can start the next day from that point.

c. Take the passage suggested in your daily reading guide. When I first became a Christian, I depended on "Our Daily Bread" devotional for my Quiet Time.

Step 3: Meditate
(Think through and soberly reflect on what you have read).

If you do not think deeply about what you are reading you will lose a major blessing of the Word of God. Paul told Timothy to think about the Word of God.

> **Consider what I say; and the Lord give thee understanding in all things.**
>
> **2 Timothy 2:7**

7 Keys for Effective Meditation

a. Read the passage slowly.

b. Do not read a very long passage unless it is necessary.

c. Stop at any verse that strikes you and think about it. God's Word is so powerful that only a single word in a verse is enough to change your life. Each quiet time should be a search for that single word that can change your life.

d. Think about the meanings of the words that you are reading.

e. Think about how the Scripture applies to life in your generation.

f.   Whisper to the Holy Spirit. Say, "Help me Holy Spirit to understand your Word. Father, give me the Spirit of Wisdom and Revelation." I have prayed for many years that God should give me the Spirit of Wisdom and Revelation of His Word.

> **That the God of our Lord Jesus Christ, the Father of glory, may give unto you the spirit of wisdom and revelation in the knowledge of him...**
>
> **Ephesians 1:17**

g. Decide on a practical way to implement the Scriptures that you have learnt. Without thinking of a way to apply the Scripture directly you will often not benefit from your quiet time.

Step 4: Move into deeper Bible study and make further references to things that strike you during your Quiet Time.

There are times that you will need to have a longer quiet time. God may minister to you about something. You must be prepared to study further. This is why it is important to have a good reference Bible.

Look through the passage again for as many of the following as possible:

i. What does the passage teach me about the nature of God: the Father, the Son, or the Holy Spirit?

ii. Is there a promise for you to believe, and so claim, taking careful note of any conditions attached?

iii. Is there a command for you to obey, or a good example for you to follow?

iv. Is there a warning for you to heed or a bad example for you to avoid?

v. Is there a prayer for you to pray or remember?

Step 5: Use your Bible reading guide.

You may refer to your daily Bible reading guide. These Bible reading guides are very helpful in developing a regular quiet time habit. You will benefit from anointed teachers whose ministry will help you to grow.

Step 6: Write down whatever the Lord tells you.

It is important to develop the habit of writing the things that God speaks to you about.

The very fact that you have acquired a notebook shows that you have faith in an invisible God. You believe that He has spoken to you and you have written down His words.

You have taken a great step of faith. Without faith it is not possible to please God.

Step 7: Now spend time praying to the Lord. Listen to the voice of the Holy Spirit.

The last step in your quiet time is to pray. At times you will pray for a short time, but there are other times you will pray for a long time. As you have your quiet time regularly, this prayer time will become longer and longer. You will soon desire longer hours with the Lord.

During the prayer time, God will speak to you through His Spirit. There are things God needs to tell you directly through His Spirit. The Holy Spirit is real and you must believe in Him as well.

CHAPTER 9

Grow in Your New Life by Praying Regularly

Prayer means talking to God. If you pray and develop a prayer life, you will grow in your relationship with God. You naturally develop a relationship with anyone you talk to often.

If for instance I preach to you, you will know what I am trying to say. But if you talk back to me, I get the chance to talk to you and you talk back to me. As this continues, the relationship becomes a little more intimate. You will begin to know me. It is the same thing with God. God has preached to us, we read out His preaching from the Bible. But if you begin to talk to Him and He talks back to you, you will develop a relationship with Him and you will know Him and He will know you.

6 Principles of Prayer

1.   **It is important to spend some time with God in prayer every day.**

Pray without ceasing.
1 Thessalonians 5:17

2.   Prayer builds you up in your faith.

But ye, beloved, building up yourselves on your most holy faith, praying in the Holy Ghost...

Jude 1:20

3.   Every Christian should pray at least 30 minutes daily when you start the habit of prayer. You should move up to praying for an hour as you grow in your daily prayer habit.

And he cometh unto the disciples, and findeth them asleep, and saith unto Peter, What, could ye not watch with me one hour?

Matthew 26:40

4.   Prayer helps you to overcome temptations.

Watch and pray, that ye enter not into temptation: the spirit indeed is willing, but the flesh is weak.

Matthew 26:41

5.   You can pray about everything.

Therefore I say unto you, What things soever ye desire, when ye pray, believe that ye receive them, and ye shall have them.

Mark 11:24

6.   You can accompany your prayer with fasting sometimes.

But thou, when thou fastest, anoint thine head, and wash thy face; That thou appear not unto men to fast, but unto thy Father which is in secret: and thy Father, which seeth in secret, shall reward thee openly.

Matthew 6:17,18

The Four Aspects of Prayer—A.C.T.S.

1. Adoration

Praise and worship God for who He is and for what He means to you. You can sing a few songs of praise and worship.

After this manner therefore pray ye: Our Father which art in heaven, Hallowed be thy name.

Matthew 6:9

Bless the Lord, O my soul: and all that is within me, bless his holy name. Bless the Lord, O my soul, and forget not all his benefits: Who forgiveth all thine iniquities; who healeth all thy diseases;

Psalm 103:1-3

2. Confession

a. Confess your sins

We must confess our sins to obtain God's forgiveness and healing for sins we commit or for things we failed to do and even for things in our hearts that we cannot see, for example pride.

If we confess our sins, he is faithful and just to forgive us our sins, and to cleanse us from all unrighteousness.

1 John 1:8,9

b. Confess your faith

We must also confess (declare, speak out) our faith in God's Word. What you believe in your heart and say with your mouth will come to pass:

For with the heart man believeth unto righteousness; and with the mouth confession is made unto salvation.

Romans 10:10

For verily I say unto you, That whosoever shall say unto this mountain, Be thou removed, and be thou cast into the sea; and shall not doubt in his heart, but shall believe that those things which he saith shall come to pass; he shall have whatsoever he saith.

Mark 11:23

As you read the Bible you would come across things God has said about His children: Who they are! What they can do! What they have! You can confess them and believe God to bring them to pass in your life. You must constantly affirm that:

I am who God says I am!

I can do what He says I can do!

I have what He says I have!

That the communication of thy faith may become effectual by the acknowledging of every good thing which is in you in Christ Jesus.

Philemon 1:6

3. Thanksgiving

a. **Thank God in all circumstances.**

In every thing give thanks: for this is the will of God in Christ Jesus concerning you.

1 Thessalonians 5:18

b. **Thank God for the things He does in your life.**

Praise ye the Lord. O give thanks unto the Lord; for he is good: for his mercy endureth for ever.

Psalm 106:1

c. Thank God in advance for what you have asked from Him but haven't yet seen.

Be careful for nothing; but in every thing by prayer and supplication with thanksgiving let your requests be made known unto God.

Philippians 4:6

4. Supplication (Asking God for your needs)

a. Ask Him for everything you need.

Ask, and it shall be given you; seek, and ye shall find; knock, and it shall be opened unto you:

Matthew 7:7

b. Ask for things concerning other people.

I exhort therefore, that, first of all, supplications, prayers, intercessions, and giving of thanks, be made for all men; For kings, and for all that are in authority; that we may lead a quiet and peaceable life in all godliness and honesty.

1 Timothy 2:1,2

CHAPTER 10

Grow as a New Believer by Fellowshipping Regularly

To grow in your new life it is important that you do not stay at home without fellowshipping. You must find a Bible-believing church and attend the services regularly.

What Is a Bible-Believing Church?

A Bible-believing church is a church where people are taught to be born again, trained to be effective Christians and the Bible is the only source of truth.

When a coal of fire is separated from the coal pot, and other burning charcoal, it dies out. Like a coal of fire you cannot survive on your own. You must fellowship with other believers to keep the Gospel fire burning in you.

Iron sharpeneth iron; so a man sharpeneth the countenance of his friend.

Proverbs 27:17

How to Develop by Fellowshipping

1.   You must go to church regularly.

Every Christian must fellowship regularly in a church, which is alive, born again, and Spirit-filled. It is very dangerous not to fellowship regularly.

Not forsaking the assembling of ourselves together, as the manner of some is; but exhorting one another: and so much the more, as ye see the day approaching.

Hebrews 10:25

Our Saviour, Jesus Christ, had the habit of going to the church of His day regularly.

And he came to Nazareth, where he had been brought up: and, as his custom was, he went into the synagogue on the sabbath day...

Luke 4:16

What happened to Judas when he kept avoiding fellowship for "legitimate" reasons?   Judas probably betrayed Christ because he often had to leave their fellowship to "sort out certain financial issues". Outside fellowship we are exposed to all sorts of temptations.

2.   You must make friends and move closely with other Christians.

You must change your friends and walk with born again Christians. You cannot do well as a Christian if you remain close to unbeliever friends.

Be not deceived: evil communications corrupt good manners.

1 Corinthians 15:33

I am a companion of all them that fear thee, and of them that keep thy precepts.

Psalm 119:63

And they continued stedfastly in the apostles' doctrine and fellowship, and in breaking of bread, and in prayers.

Acts 2:42

CHAPTER 11

Develop the Art of Witnessing and Soulwinning

1. We must tell our friends about what has happened to us in Christ. Your friends may come to know Christ because of your testimony. The woman of Samaria became a soul-winner when she met Christ.

    The woman then left her waterpot, and went her way into the city, and saith to the men, Come, see a man, which told me all things that ever I did: is not this the Christ? Then they went out of the city, and came unto him... And many of the Samaritans of that city believed on him for the saying of the woman, which testified, He told me all that ever I did.

    John 4:28-30,39

2. It is an important public declaration that shows that you are not ashamed of Christ before men.

    Whosoever therefore shall be ashamed of me and of my words in this adulterous and sinful generation; of him also shall the Son of man be ashamed, when he cometh in the glory of his Father with the holy angels.

    Mark 8:38

For I am not ashamed of the gospel of Christ: for it is the power of God unto salvation to every one that believeth; to the Jew first, and also to the Greek.

Romans 1:16

3. **It is our responsibility as Christians to tell others about the truth.**

When I say unto the wicked, O wicked man, thou shalt surely die; if thou dost not speak to warn the wicked from his way, that wicked man shall die in his iniquity; but his blood will I require at thine hand. Nevertheless, if thou warn the wicked of his way to turn from it; if he do not turn from his way, he shall die in his iniquity; but thou hast delivered thy soul.

Ezekiel 33:8,9

And he said unto them, Go ye into all the world, and preach the gospel to every creature.

Mark 16:15

And Jesus came and spake unto them, saying, All power is given unto me in heaven and in earth. Go ye therefore, and teach all nations, baptizing them in the name of the Father, and of the Son, and of the Holy Ghost: Teaching them to observe all things whatsoever I have commanded you: and, lo, I am with you alway, even unto the end of the world. Amen.

Matthew 28:18-20

But ye shall receive power, after that the Holy Ghost is come upon you: and ye shall be witnesses unto me both in Jerusalem, and in all Judaea, and in Samaria, and unto the uttermost part of the earth.

Acts 1:8

4.   You must bear fruit.

Ye have not chosen me, but I have chosen you, and ordained you, that ye should go and bring forth fruit, and that your fruit should remain: that whatsoever ye shall ask of the Father in my name, he may give it you.

John 15:16

CHAPTER 12

Your Role as a Church Member

1. Your first role in the church is that of a faithful attendee.

Decide to attend all services, meetings and special programmes organized by the church. Just as you cannot eat once a month and say that you have enough food, you can also not come to church once a while and think that you have enough fellowship.

Moreover it is required in stewards, that a man be found faithful.

1 Corinthians 4:2

Faithful means constant, regular, reliable, dedicated and committed.

2. Your second role in the church is that of a stable Christian.

You must be planted in a local church and be established there. Do not form the habit of roaming from one church to the other seeking signs and wonders or other solutions.

For example, a student on campus does not study medicine today, law tomorrow, and geography the next day. He will gain nothing and achieve nothing in the end. It is important to be stable in one place.

The righteous shall flourish like the palm tree: he shall grow like a cedar in Lebanon. Those that be planted in the house of the Lord shall flourish in the courts of our God.

Psalm 92:12,13

3.   Your third role is to pay your tithes.

Giving your tithes (ten percent of your income) regularly every month or whenever you receive income.

Honour the Lord with thy substance, and with the firstfruits of all thine increase: So shall thy barns be filled with plenty, and thy presses shall burst out with new wine.

Proverbs 3:9,10

Bring ye all the tithes into the storehouse, that there may be meat in mine house, and prove me now herewith, saith the Lord of hosts, if I will not open you the windows of heaven, and pour you out a blessing, that there shall not be room enough to receive it.

Malachi 3:10

The tithes will support the church financially to help carry the Gospel to others who have not heard and to keep the church work running. God will bless and prosper you as you support His work. Allow Jesus to be Lord over your finances as well.

4.   Your fourth role is to give offerings.

Give, and it shall be given unto you; good measure, pressed down, and shaken together, and running over, shall men give into your bosom. For with the same

measure that ye mete withal it shall be measured to
you again.

Luke 6:38

5.   Your fifth role is to make your talents and gifts
available to the church.

Put your God-given abilities to full use in His house. God
has given everyone an ability or talent that is beneficial to His
church. Do not hide your abilities!   Be ready to perform any
special duties assigned to you by the leadership.

6.   Your sixth role is to know your pastors, love and
respect them.

   a. Know your pastors.

   And we beseech you, brethren, to know them which
   labour among you, and are over you in the Lord, and
   admonish you;

1 Thessalonians 5:12

   b. Respect your pastors.

   And to esteem them very highly in love for their work's
   sake. And be at peace among yourselves.

1 Thessalonians 5:13

   c. Believe in your pastors.

   ...Hear me, O Judah, and ye inhabitants of Jerusalem;
   Believe in the Lord your God, so shall ye be established;
   believe his prophets, so shall ye prosper.

2 Chronicles 20:20

   d. Pray for your pastors.

   Brethren, pray for us.

1 Thessalonians 5:25

Finally, brethren, pray for us, that the word of the Lord may have free course, and be glorified, even as it is with you:

2 Thessalonians 3:1

Pray for us: for we trust we have a good conscience, in all things willing to live honestly.

Hebrews 13:18

7.   **Your seventh role is to bear fruit in Christ.**

Ye have not chosen me, but I have chosen you, and ordained you, that ye should go and bring forth fruit, and that your fruit should remain: that whatsoever ye shall ask of the Father in my name, he may give it you.

John 15:16

After being born again it is important to bear fruit. Jesus saved you and you must show your appreciation by doing something for the kingdom of God. Seek the kingdom of God first and all other things will be added onto you. Let Matthew 6:33 be the greatest key to success in your life.

But seek ye first the kingdom of God, and his righteousness; and all these things shall be added unto you.

Matthew 6:33

With these master keys, you will be established in Jesus Christ. One day, you will be glad that you knew Jesus and you grew up spiritually. May you be rooted and grounded in Christ until He comes again!